Nameless Boy

ALSO BY DOUGLAS GOETSCH

Your Whole Life*
The Job of Being Everybody
What's Worse*
First Time Reading Freud*
Nobody's Hell
Wherever You Want*

*chapbooks

Nameless Boy

Douglas Goetsch

Diana

ORCHISES
Washington

Library of Congress Cataloguing-in-Publication Data

Goetsch, Douglas.
  [Poems. Selections]
  Nameless boy / Douglas Goetsch.
    pages ; cm
  ISBN 978-1-932535-31-0 (alk. paper)
  I. Title.
  PS3557.O3226A6 2015
  811'.54--dc23
                                    2014017767

Orchises Press
P.O. Box 320533
Alexandria, VA 22320-4533

G 6 E 4 C 2

for William Zinsser

ACKNOWLEDGMENTS

Thanks to the editors of the following magazines, where these poems, some in previous versions, originally appeared:

Arcadia: "On the School Bus"
Alabama Literary Review: "1989," "At the Residence," "One Good
    Thing," "Simple Math," "Telemachus at 50," "Too Soon"
The Gettysburg Review: "Black People Can't Swim," "Pee on Your
    Foot," "People," "Privilege," "Upstairs"
Hartskill Review: "The Brides of Rome," "Walking a Labyrinth"
Margie: "To a Teacher," "Wisdom's Passing"
New Ohio Review: "Back Flip," "Joe's Tax," "Love Songs," "Mexico,"
    "Mrs. Morganstern's Cocktail Party," "Today's World"
The New Yorker: "Different Dogs," "Poem"
Numéro Cinq: "Elaine!"
Plume: "Flash Flood," "Shin Issues," "Swimming to New Zealand"
Rattle: "Nameless Boy," "Recess"
Slipstream: "Bill"
The Southern Review: "Forgiveness Poem," "You Could"
Verse Wisconsin: "The Ripple in Your Day"

Five poems from this collection were published in the chapbook *Your
Whole Life* (Slipstream Press)

"Black People Can't Swim" appeared in *The Pushcart Prize XXXVI: Best
of the Small Presses*

Thanks to these wise and helpful readers: Peter Murphy, Sarah Pettit,
Roger Lathbury, Mark Halliday, Jill Rosser, Tony Hoagland, Stephen
Dunn, Baron Wormser, Hayan Charara, Alvaro Cardona-Hine, Mary
Ruefle, Rick Jackson, Betsy Sholl

Thanks to the National Endowment for the Arts for a poetry fellow-
ship that helped in the completion of this book.

CONTENTS

1

2

3

4

Some people get born with the wrong name, wrong parents. That happens.

– *Bob Dylan*

1

Poem

You've probably right away noticed
the title of this poem is "Poem"
and that's because this is exactly
what I plan on writing—in fact
I've already begun, sort of.
I still need to find a subject
for such a serious theme—
nothing too trivial or self-conscious.
We've all read poems called "Poem"
about would-be lovers or piebald foals,
levitating saints or the flowering
of transplanted trees and I
figure a poem called "Poem"
ought to be about something
likewise worthy and dignified. But all that
sort of stuff seems to be taken.
After finding a topic (we haven't
but it's more important to keep
the damn thing moving) next up
is the proper tone, which can't be
too solemn—that's been covered
by folks like Thomas Hardy
who let's face it I'm not gonna top—
but also not too clever, some middle
ground, tattooed chemo-nurse
or stepmom-at-a-rifle-range type
of deal. We don't for example
want this poetry professor who's
been at the lectern the past hour

attempting to detonate himself
with hip locutions in
between grey mastodons of verbiage,
proving he's down with Motown despite
being so freakishly erudite.
In the midst of his many-sectioned opus
on the history of the human condition,
somewhere between Pol Pot
and the advent of the bikini,
I begin wishing he would instead
read us a poem about his embarrassing
throwing arm, on display at second base
in the poetry vs. prose softball game
at the MFA picnic. The fact
that he's six four made it all
the more heartbreaking and I
wondered, as the ball died
in the dirt well short of first,
as creative non-fiction writers circled the bases,
how he survived his childhood.
Was there a father or uncle on the scene
to stave off the catastrophe,
hurling fast balls and *attaboys*
in the backyard while Mother
peeked through kitchen blinds?
Were schoolyard bullies happy
to assist with his emasculation,
or did he have kind friends, a cohort
of thoughtful children with international parents

who cared about politics and dance
         and used star fruit in their cooking?
     Or was it poetry that led to him
       being able to move in the world,
    marry, reproduce and take
the field, pound a mitt and be
      naked among the people he loves?

Mexico

All these people going to Mexico and not coming back...
you only hear about them on Facebook or in blogs
because they're in Mexico. Some of them try
to get you to come down there and hang with them,
as though Mexico were some kind of cult they joined,
though perhaps they're just lonely, though not lonely
enough to come back from Mexico, yet some reappear
temporarily, like people stepping out of a rave
for a water break. You notice their hair matted into dreads
and their eyes glazed, more of their whites showing,
giving them a surprised blown out spooky calm look.
They never talk about what they *do* in Mexico.
It is as though the space below the border were a narrative
black hole from which no linear story can escape—
except those of the brilliant Cormac McCarthy, who
is from East Tennessee, a black hole of a different sort.
I hope I haven't offended anyone here.
I suppose this little riff on Mexico could seem
a tad ignorant, though we know the real Mexico
has nothing to do with anything I say. I just set out to say
Mexico a lot. Seriously, that's it. Everyone gets so
hung up on words, on account of them having meanings—
but *do* they? If this were music, and instead of *Mexico*
I wrote an E flat for the horn section, could anyone
possibly have a problem with that? Or if this were
a painting, and *Mexico* was just a kind of brushstroke
I was trying, a blob of magenta smeared across a canvas,
who would take umbrage at that? Even if Andy Warhol
painted it—although knowing Warhol that

magenta smear would be Richard Nixon's lipstick.
I wouldn't mind going to Mexico myself, rent a big place
on the outskirts of a town named after a saint,
get to know the villagers, figure out the drinking
water situation, how to steer clear of local justice,
how much Spanish it takes to get a woman.
Then I'd invite *you* down to join me. *You gotta
come to Mexico!* I'd say, though I wouldn't say
much else, just that it was someplace quiet
and amazingly inexpensive, where you sleep a lot
and wear the same pants for days, a place
from which no news gets out, even if it tried,
a place you thought was only in your mind.

Mrs. Morganstern's Cocktail Party

"You're gonna need this someday at a cocktail party!"
crowed Mrs. Morganstern, tiny lady with a helmet
of dyed red hair scribbling Africa facts
across the blackboard, going toe to toe with teens
contesting the likelihood of her daily claim—
though I, for one, was more apt to dream
of a future rife with cocktail parties,
porcelain-skinned women in feathery gowns
wafting through high-ceilinged rooms
full of artists, scholars, film moguls
and me: shoulder to shoulder
with my disadvantaged peers, who lacked the benefit
of 8th grade history with Mrs. Morganstern.

Though now, well into middle age, I would
like to ask Mrs. Morganstern: where the hell
was the cocktail party? Did the world turn
a corner between her generation and mine,
placing a moratorium on the highball,
swapping it for the kegger, quarts of Miller
in the woods behind Main Street, upside-down
kamikazes on frat party couches, the table
at the back wall of the literary reading
where tight-assed professors spewed classical
allusions to girls with daddy issues while sucking
down cups of boxed wine? And while I didn't
mind clinking those little mugs
at sawdust-strewn McSorleys with the Department
Chair who kept saying, "I love my wife" more

and more the drunker he got,
       it wasn't Mrs. Morganstern's cocktail party,

        the one where I meet *my* wife, all because
    the right moment arose for me to deliver
           a morsel I've been carrying since 8th grade:
"Funny thing: it was actually under the leadership of Jomo Kenyatta
     that Kenya was able to shrug off colonialism
       while remaining stable and prosperous"—
whereupon a waifish beauty named Candace or Muriel—
           no: *Giselle!*—pulls back her hair, leans in
and whispers, "Who *are* you?"

      And what of Mrs. Morganstern, who I think of every
        time I hear the song "Goodnight, Irene"—
for that was her first name: Irene. 13-year-olds
          aren't supposed to know that, but we did
because Mrs. Morganstern didn't care about
     such things, compared to how she loved history.
        And she loved us—otherwise, she wouldn't have
    attended the junior high prom each spring,
         and she wouldn't have done The Bump
with Stuart Vargas, the biggest trouble-
     maker in the class, squatting lower and lower
       and knocking asses, as that dance is done.

Upstairs

I am carrying a boy who fell asleep in the car
upstairs. This isn't in itself unusual—nothing
in itself is. I could be rushing downstairs
in another house cradling a Yorkshire Terrier,
but that's not how things have worked out.
The boy isn't mine—though for the moment
I guess he is. He's big for six. I need to grip
him tight. He has wooly hair and dark
alert eyes when he's awake. He can't stand
girls, and likes a little of his mother's pink
polish on his toes. Earlier, at the rest stop,
he and his brother played Rock, Paper, Scissors,
only it was *Rock, Paper, Scissors, Black Hole!*
which they cried, crashing into each other,
or *Rock, Paper, Scissors, Supernova!* or *Atom Bomb!*—
whatever disaster they could think up to trump
all previous disasters, though nothing to match
their father collapsed dead on the back deck
in his barbecue apron, or them being whisked
from the sight, as John Kennedy's children
undoubtedly were, by some wise and quick-
thinking soul, perhaps to a room upstairs—
these stairs I'm walking up now, three years
later with a boy sleeping deeply. If you've never
done what I am doing and get the opportunity,
I would recommend it. You might find
you've never stepped quite so purposefully,
as though climbing out of life's trouble
into a cloud realm, and laying down
a body that could be anyone's.

Love Songs

At 12 Richard Perry came from California
to throw a football way further than anyone
on the block. If that's the kind of thing
you admire—and we did—you could also
admire other things about him, even his stutter,
which manifested in the huddle when he drew
plays on his man-sized palms, his intelligent eyes
signaling some clever maneuver moments
before the words for it emerged, creating
a kind of charmed suspense, while the defense
waited hands on hips. I was his favorite receiver,
always going long, all through the fall, winter,
into spring, where one day, after several
blinks, Richard stated the following:
"Love songs are the best songs there are."
Four 12-year-olds looked at each other, then back at
Richard, who broke the huddle without a play.
Later we would find out he had a girl—
Regina Eiselstein, from the other side
of the highway—and though his assertion
about love songs seemed way out of line,
isn't it always the case with that kind of feeling,
that you have to tell everyone? Personally
I found love songs boring and stupid, like
watching my parents play bridge, but that
was also his point: to tell us something
we couldn't know. And I wish now I could
have surrendered to something the way
Richard Perry gave it up completely,
something I didn't do at age 12 or 20

or even 40. I've never shocked anyone
with a confession that strange and tender,
stuttered without embarrassment because
he had love, he had Regina and a song
in his head that he knew was worth more
than his rocket arm which could launch
footballs into the sky. And in case you haven't
figured it out this is all about you.
You, Julie, spiraling into my arms
like a pass that's been traveling 30 years,
like a song I can finally hear.

Recess

A ring of children seated Indian style,
     a girl deciding which head to tap
         as she orbits them in her pretty dress

saying *Duck Duck Duck Duck Duck.*
     Every boy wants to be the goose,
         to bolt up and run down this girl

before she makes it around
     to the spot he vacated. Once
         they saw her trip and fall, exposing

a lovely backside covered in lace.
     Maybe that is why their heads rise
         like charmed snakes as she passes

saying *Duck Duck Duck Duck Duck,*
     annoying the girls in the circle, who frown,
         and attracting now the attention

of their teacher, leaning against a tree,
     bringing her gaze down from the clouds
         where she had been pondering two men—

the one she recently broke up with
     filling her with regret about the much
         better, more beautiful one from college.

Now she is twenty-nine, on perhaps
    the last warm day of September,
        the smartest, prettiest girl in the class

is going *Duck Duck Duck Duck Duck*
    in an endless left-hand turn,
        and she can't figure out whether

the girl is powerful or helpless,
    as she blinks back tears and blows
    the whistle to end this.

Black People Can't Swim

When I told Patricia how much I loved the pool at the Y
she said, "Oh, black people can't swim,"
which made me grateful to be let in on this,
not the information, but the intimacy—
the fact that she could let fly with such a piece
of black on black attitude without the slightest
bit of shame or self-consciousness. We were in
a bar, me and five black women who were paying
more attention than any white females
I'd ever seen to a football game on TV.
The injured halfback in elegant street clothes
towering above the sideline reporter
caused each woman to suck her teeth—
"That is one fine brother."
"Best thing I'll *never* have sex with."
"The lips are a little big, but homeboy still pretty."
"Why wouldn't you have sex with him?" I asked.
"Cause he a ho," Halle said.
"Everyone in the NFL's a ho," Cheryl and E.J. chimed in.
I looked up at the TV again and this player,
whose name I'd known, now seemed changed
into someone both simpler and deeper.
We were all toddlers when Martin dreamed
of little black children and little white children
going to school arm in arm. He dreamed this too:
a restaurant table where we were free to reveal
not just our true, but our mysterious, irrational selves

in the presence of the other tribe without apology.
So here was Kaiasia, who had given us a lecture
on how *not* to pronounce her name, and who held
my arm all meal saying I was her husband.
"What was *that?*" they asked when she left.
A mystery. Earlier, on the walk over, she pulled me
away from the group into a leather shop
to show me a $200 Italian bag on layaway.
"And what did you say?"
"Nice bag."
"That's not what she wanted to hear."
"Which was?"
They eyed each other, deciding who would tell:
"Honey, when a sister shows a man something
on layaway she wants him to buy it."
"No way—" but they were all nodding, and I had to
love this country, or this ten square feet of it,
where they could tell me about men and women
and race and layaway. And I could have told them
about all the black people who swim at the Y,
though maybe they already knew
and just delighted in saying with impunity
what the vice president of the Los Angeles Dodgers
blurted out on national TV. "They don't
have the buoyancy," Al Campanis told Ted Koppel,
then promptly lost his job, and rightfully so.

Different Dogs

I'm sitting here with this bony little Doberman
atop a stinky knoll in back of the Oklahoma
City Animal Shelter. I make sure to walk
the wretched ones. The others barked
raucously as she ambled out of her cage
into the noose of my leash, which hung slack
as we shuffled past the monsters in the segregated pen—
some, the workers say, are just born bad.
This dog trembles in the fall chill as we watch
a mist drift over the downtown skyline.
Somewhere in that fog is Krystal, the woman
I met Saturday night, who seemed to know
everybody in the bar, but kept circling back
to me, even after she let some crazy asshole
lick her eyeball. At closing time she gave me
her number, and I figured, doing the math,
her younger age and good breasts plus nice face
minus the acne scars, which didn't matter
to me, but probably did to her, equaled
my first Oklahoma girl. But when I called
she talked only about herself, her careers,
her degrees, her deep spirituality, her power
to literally make the sun come out whenever
she felt like it. I thought she was just
misusing the word *literally*, as often happens,
but no, she meant it, and if I were younger
I'd have challenged her, but instead I just got
depressed, more depressed after the sex.
Better to be here with this miserable dog

watching the clouds roll in. She's leaning
against me now, and I can't help but pat her
grubby shoulder, rest my chin on her head.
When dogs gaze out in the same direction
as you, sniffing the wind, they seem to know
the future. They don't tell you, when you're
a volunteer, which ones got destroyed,
which got adopted. You just show up
and find different dogs in the cages.

Joe's Tax

Are we ever more innocent than when doing taxes?
I'm not talking about how we rob the country
by deducting the case of **Alpo** we bought

on Take Your Dog To Work Day, but just the helpless
look on our faces, the week-end in early spring
we're hunkered down at a desk or kitchen table

strewn with receipts and instructions
from a government so much bigger than us,
hovering in space like a circle of priests.

Even if we believe every hair is numbered,
who could possibly account for a year without
fudging, our glasses slipping down our noses

as we wonder which cab rides, how many square
feet of our home, what percentage of a phone bill
was *business?* I know a man who wrote off dates

with women, restaurant checks, gifts of chocolate
and flowers, and when they audited him he said
he was a love poet conducting research—

he even brought along one of his books.
My grandpa loved to recount the year
he dumped a shoebox full of receipts

on the tax man's desk, threw up his arms
and said, "Knock yourself out!"
Even if you rendered unto Caesar, the IRS

could still be waiting for you at the gates.
Here I've claimed $3400 in psychotherapy bills
under "Medical" expenses, but *can* I?

Joe will know. Joe at *Joe's Tax* in Brooklyn
where I'll take the F train tomorrow and sit
half the day in a storefront where a sign reads

This is a waiting room. If you are not prepared
to wait then you are in the wrong room.
Joe works with his wife, son and six others

on a sort of platform a few steps up, where
everyone hears everything, so I hope he
doesn't bring up the $3400 for psychotherapy.

The customers with their stubs and papers
look like ancient children outside
the principal's office. Last year we all

watched a guy break into a happy dance
when he found out he was getting a refund.
Barry Manilow's "Copacabana" blasted from

somewhere, Joe's wife handed the man
a pair of blinking neon glasses, videotaped
him on her smart phone and posted it

to YouTube before Joe could say, *Next!*
That's what I'd call good therapy, or religion,
or maybe just a full accounting.

Back Flip

I bet I could do a back flip right now.
I've got a feeling they're not as hard
as we think. They're just dangerous.
I'm thinking of going for it right here
in my living room, with no witness
except for the dog, who enjoys watching
me practice Tai Chi, as my wife walks
through snickering, "What're you going
to do, inner peace 'em to death?"

Let's say I walk into an appliance store
where two men are stealing televisions
and I do a back flip, causing one
of them to turn to the other and say
through his ski mask, "Why do you think
that bald guy did a back flip?"
and in that moment of hesitation
the authorities swoop in to *nab* them.
Or what if I were caught
in an embarrassing lie at a dinner party
and instead of trying to explain myself
I calmly stepped away from the table and
executed a back flip, causing my friends
to remark, "What an unusual thing for *Doug*
to do. I wouldn't have expected that." Thus
revealing a facet of myself more worthy
of discussion than the embarrassment
moments earlier, all because of a back flip

which, as I say, I could probably do right now—
and even if you doubt such a claim, we know
it's at least *possible,* not like when we were kids
tying curtains around our necks and sprinting
across the backyard pretending to be Superman.
There was a boy in the news who believed
so hard he could fly they found him
in a Superman costume with his arms
outstretched at the bottom of a quarry.
Anyway I'm saying a back flip is possible—
more than possible, for I have maintained
bodily flexibility through my 30s
and into my 40s, plus I'm generally good
at committing to things, which I'm guessing
would be a key to effective back flipping.

I see it as no harder than the leap
your average television detective makes
from one rooftop to another—which only
seems like a big deal because it's high up,
plus they're wearing suits and ties, the pursuit
of criminals being a formal occasion.
Anyhow I think I could cover that
no problemo—not only me but you too,
and that's my point: *a lot* of us could
do a back flip. We just *don't know it!*
We have *no idea* what we are capable of
and this is how the world keeps us in check—
everyone except for the stunt men,

and the ones who run off and join the circus,
or tear up their passports and go native,
or change their sex and become lounge singers,
or stand their ground in front of a tank.
If I do this back flip there's no telling
what I'll do next. Or maybe I'll keep it
a secret, and remain an ordinary civilian,
humble and quiet as I've been,
though with the knowledge
of what I'm capable of
buzzing inside me.

People

Who are all these *people...*
ducking into boutiques, bouncing out
of cafés, younger, taller than ever—
Generation *Dude*? Generation
type w/my thumbs? We used to be
them, of course, only they don't
have quite our panache, our cast
of characters; their dreams seem
so counterfeit; their exploits
pale in comparison to ours

as ours pale in comparison to the
madcap hijinks of the Rat Pack—
that jazz-crooning, highball-drinking,
fedora-wearing, celebrity-roasting,
mafioso-befriending, skirt-
chasing, ingénue-divorcing
cadre of song-and-dance men
that owned the strip and
ruled the night from Vegas
to Hollywood to Broadway,

predated, in turn, by young John Keats
and his circle of loyal Cockneys—
Brown, Hunt, Haslam, Severn—
who defended their bright star
from epically stupid critics,
and risked their lives to be with him
when he was coughing blood,

while Percy Shelley wrote from Italy
offering to nurse his rival—
a shimmering of humanity

that could never hope to rival
the 10,000-year sliver of time
in which a late Neanderthal spied
an early *Homo sapiens* across a clover field,
regarding the humble hominid
of smaller head and smoother brow
with what had to be an emotion
unprecedented in human, or non-
human history, uttering (more or less)
"Who the fuck are you?"

2

Wisdom's Passing

for the students of Webb School, Knoxville, TN

The first time I heard about the tree in the forest
I was in 8th grade music class.
Short, plump, goateed Mr. Warner

drew a giant ear, a felled trunk and said,
There is no sound unless I'm there to hear it.
Then paused so we could write that in our notebooks.

Andy Schecter wrote, *How the hell can he know?*
tore out the page and passed it around.
Poor Mr. Warner, overmatched by 13-year-olds

who use, not arguments, but infallible
bullshit detectors, on tilt since the day
he read from his unfinished dissertation

on The Beatles, stopping for us to copy
his words verbatim. Down the hall
Mr. Stetbacher told his Social Studies class

there were only three races of people—
Caucasian, African, and "Mongoloid"—
which made the two Puerto Ricans in the school

feel even more left out. It was hard to tell
Stetbacher's race—his face looked white
but his afro was big and tight enough

to catch pencils. To us he was more fat
than anything. Mr. Hamdallah
was Palestinian, whatever that was.

Never take a job off the books—his advice,
repeated daily, was all we could hear
through his accent. I can't recall what subject

he taught, neither could he, but it's hard to dislike
a man who sings "Pennies from Heaven" as he
enters the room every day drunk on life.

Miss Bix, the new health teacher all the boys
and even some of the girls wanted to bone,
tried desperately and unsuccessfully to get us

to believe rape had nothing to do with sex.
I'm thankful for these dedicated teachers,
men and women who forced us to reach

our own conclusions, theirs being so asinine,
fostering self-trust, so we could tackle
the important questions of our age:

whether Rebecca Flanagan had hairy armpits,
if the redhead on the Aviance perfume
commercial was really Mike Burton's mom,

and why Pete Falciano, who could bench the universal,
showed up each Monday with new bruises—
questions you couldn't find answers to in any book.

As for Mr. Warner, he went on to complete
his research on the overrated rock group,
put a *Dr.* in front his name, and put that name

at the top of a column he penned for the local
gazette, sharing truths only he seemed
to possess, such as how the Vietnam War

spawned a new generation of homosexuals
by depriving boys of their fathers.
He called the column "Wisdom's Passing"—

and it certainly was, long before Reagan
said, *Facts are stupid things,* before Clinton
didn't inhale, and before everyone declared

a *War on Terror*—as if you could
bomb an idea, any more than you can
silence a falling forest with a theory.

Today's World

Just now I thought of: wainscoting.
I thought: well there's something
we don't normally think about. Go ahead
and click on your 900 satellite channels,
see if anyone *breathes* the word.
Surely there was a day when wainscoting was all the rage.
It might have been in the time of Charlotte Bronte
or William Makepeace Thackeray. I haven't
read any of their novels, but I'd be surprised
if they didn't make it a point to include wainscoting—
or a conspicuous *lack thereof*—in their
voluminous descriptions of interiors, rooms
where young governesses in layers of skirts
sit quietly waiting... thinking of the seaside
summers of their youth, then suddenly paling
at the prospect of spinsterhood, years of muted light
staring at wainscoting—or *the* wainscoting.
I don't actually know what wainscoting is,
not *technically*. I could sit here and bullshit you,
or I could look it up on the internet, but that's
not the point. The point is once there was a world
before wainscoting—a barbaric place, though
not, I imagine, without a certain raw beauty—
followed by a transitional period, an age
of incipient wainscoting, *as it were,* marked by
the usual stumbles and false steps, giving way
to the tastefully wainscoted *milieu* of Charlotte Bronte
and William Makepeace Thackeray, which brings us
to today's world of zip drives and smoothies

and people from Sector 6. Now you can get
replacement applicator tips at Bed Bath & Beyond,
or boot shapers—keep your favorite boots from sagging—
but you can no longer find wainscoting,
at least I don't *think* you can...

The Ripple in Your Day

I'd like to pull back the hair from your face
and ask how you get through the ripple in your day,
the one that comes unannounced
like a feral animal sitting on the lawn
facing your windows—you'd think
you'd be used to it by now. It stays
maybe a minute, maybe an hour,
and doesn't go away until it does.
Do you settle into your favorite chair
with the universal remote, spend an hour
in the shower, bury your head
in crosswords, sleep in your clothes?
Do you buy crap on eBay, Google
people from your old school, picturing
the days they're having in other cities?
Does coffee deliver you, perhaps
an early cocktail, a spoon and a half-
gallon of cookie dough ice cream?
Maybe you scream at Customer Service,
or research how to make a bomb.
Painkillers would be refreshingly direct.
Are you one of those who can stare
at themselves in the mirror and pronounce
affirmations? Do you pray,
or do you put on a certain song and sway
empty-handed in the darkening room?

What is it that you do, do every day,
that everybody does, even heroes

on posters in our childhood bedrooms—
athletes, rock stars, Hollywood A-listers
who, if they don't make it past the ripple
in their day, end up in the papers,
drunk in their driveways, wandering nameless
in Orange County, found motionless
on their made beds or in their bathrooms.
Cloistered nuns, Henry Kissinger, people
in the People's Republic of China—
everybody's day, even their best day,
has a ripple, when something reverses,
dust motes float slowly upward
and memories of old wounds
trudge into the room like wet dogs.
Have you come to believe the ripple is you?
The ripple isn't you. How you
get through it—that's not even you,
it's just your life, your story, the story
of us all, each inside our own day,
and *with* you, though feeling so separate
and holding on. Holding on.

Flash Flood

I don't want to die. Not on a day
that's cloudy or clear, near women
pretty or plain, listening to the song
of a sparrow or a truck backing up,
or the Roberta Flack tune I belt out
under cover of an arriving train.
Not while falling in love or breaking up,
or doing both at the same time, as rain
pours off the café awning, and baristas
in their aprons scramble to get
bowls under all the leaks. I don't want it
to stop. I feel I've been alive
less than the seven days allotted the housefly.
Whatever I've read about death,
whatever I believed about past lives,
parallel universes, the eternal—just forget it.
There's no world but this one,
no river to cross, no other
side to see you on.

On the School Bus

My brother stands at the white line,
three steep steps above the open door,
his chest, through his coat, pressed
against a long bony arm barring his way.
The arm belongs to old Toothless,
the substitute bus driver who earlier
asked if anyone knew the route,
and my brother came forward to sit
in front, where the girls sit, and direct him
over the turnpike, under the expressway,
past schools in other towns, until
Toothless realized he'd been hijacked.
Now we're at our stop, it's getting dark,
and he intends to keep my brother
on the bus, take him back to wherever
they keep the buses. My brother says
that's illegal on account of he's a minor.
Toothless grabs a fistful of his coat
and flings him into a seat back so hard
it shocks us all. I watch my brother
wipe a tear, before he bolts back
to the line and heaves his violin
out the bus door, onto the Murphy's lawn,
the case popping open, the instrument
tumbling out and sliding to a halt
on a patch of thawing snow.
"Look what you made me do!" he says,
"Now I got to go out and get that."
I don't know what got into my brother

that day, how he went from being a jerk
and poor practitioner of a faggy instrument,
to someone we had to grudgingly admire,
if only for the fact that none of us was sure
we had the balls to do—whether we'd ever
want to or not—what he did, what he
was about to do. But I have to leave him here—
pressed against old Toothless's arm—because
I don't remember what happened next.

I'm sorry, but how many of us recall exactly
how we got home from all our trouble?
We're only sure we lived, we managed
somehow to follow one breath with another
until suddenly, unbelievably, we were
older people: you, me, Toothless.
Though not my brother: he's still
stuck on that bus, scared and defiant,
and maybe I keep him there. Whenever
I want to see past my hatred for him—
the bullying, the mop of dark hair
bobbing in laughter each time I was beaten—
I think of that violin in the snow.

1989

I woke each day to the same couple of songs
on my radio alarm, due no doubt
to the alchemy of programming format,
though it felt more like Groundhog Day—
6:05, and Randy Travis still *waiting*
for you to forgive me, but you
keep saying you can't even start...
Or "Kokomo," that ode to tropical paradise—
Aruba, Jamaica, ooh I wanna take ya...
Anywhere but here, a rooming house of men
I never spoke to, beneath a slate sky excreting ice
and sleet all through March. I trudged back
and forth to a job that had me so stressed
and tired even my clothes wanted to quit.
My only solace: re-runs of *Hill Street Blues,*
that lovable band of dysfunctional cops—
Andy Renko bickering in his Southern drawl
with Bobby Hill, his black partner,
alcoholic Norman Buntz who rode alone,
little Mick Belker hauling in perps like a dog
dragging in road kill, sweet Sergeant Esterhaus
pronouncing the benediction with that long
pointed finger: "Let's be careful out there."
It didn't air till midnight, and kept me up till 12:55,
when, once again, the beautiful public defender
and the smart precinct captain climbed into bed
after a day at each other's throats, to laugh
and tease and touch like teenagers.
Then five hours of sleep before The Beach Boys

chimed in from *A little place like Kokomo—*
we'll get there fast, and then we'll take it slow—
and I wished that magnificent wall of sound
could hold back the day, wished I could fall
forever in Randy Travis's high lonesome
like a stone you have picked up and thrown
to the hard rock bottom of your heart.
I don't know how I managed, each morning,
to reach over and turn off that radio,
peel back the covers, get up, dress
in the dark tunnel of a life so desolate.
I mean that: I don't know how I did it.
I don't know how anyone does.

One Good Thing

Who knows how
you've gotten here,
but you can always
do one good thing.
In fact, you should.
Wash a dish or
water a plant.
That's not nothing.

We're not talking
about paying the bills,
or even changing
a light bulb, but maybe
that underwear
finds the hamper?

Just one thing.
Then rest awhile.

Soon you might be
up for a shower,
or egg salad.
But this isn't a race,
so take it easy.

But don't watch TV.
If you do, not the news.
You already know enough
of other people's trouble,

or achievements—what
Mandela or Gandhi did—
and you're not on
some march to the sea.

This is more about
making the bed
and putting socks on.
Basic stuff, in sequence,
like breathing out
before breathing in.

You've got a right.
You're on this earth,
for whatever reason,
with nothing to
apologize for—at least
nothing today, so far.

The Brides of Rome

On weekends, all spring: weddings
           throughout the old city, bridal parties
                     fanned out on the steps
of 900 ancient churches,
           from San Giovanni in Laterano
                     to Santa Maria Maggiore,
from Santa Maria della Pace
           to Santa Maria del Popolo,
                     the flustered photographers
waving and shooing children,
           overwrought mothers, tearful
                     aunts, the fathers' hands
stuffed in pockets,
           the groomsmen slicking back
                     their hair, the bridesmaids
tossing theirs, and glancing
           sidelong, aching for a role
                     in some afternoon plot.
At the center of the universe,
           framed by pin curls
                     and a cyclone of white lace,
the eyes of the bride glow like coals,
           causing, for a moment, all
                     of Rome to pale to gray—
birds in the pines,
           rooftops crammed with antennas,
                     underwear on the lines,
and people, most destined
           never, or never again
                     to be a bride—

gypsies, fishmongers, pilgrim nuns,
    Renaissance graffiti artists,
        pizza-munching tourists,
machine gun-toting Carabinieri,
    drivers of little Fiats
        tearing down cobblestone
straightaways where
    children play soccer
        with a soup can.
The rank and file of the human
    pageant, which all too soon
        the brides of Rome
will rejoin, and resume their places
    on the Felliniesque
        conveyor belt of toilers
in factories, hagglers at market,
    cheek-pinchers at christenings,
        widows at gravesites.
Even now, with smiles
    bright as the camera flash,
        they're on their way—
already beginning
    to disintegrate into
        dust on stone walls
full of cherubs
    who have spied
        on how many Sundays
for how many springs,
    how many women and
        how many men,

spilling out
    the doors and
        down the steps?

At the Residence

Every odd morning, in the small hours,
they see the paramedics rolling up
with sirens off. "Lucky stiff," they say,
all through breakfast—dying in your sleep
better than hitting the Lotto. And so
they wander off to nap in the day room,
courtyard, barber shop. Even nap-proud Leo
gives it a go, like a baby in a carriage
hoping to get stolen. The other chief
activity: complaints about the food—
Who could possibly survive on this?
The staff helped organize a food committee,
they died (lucky stiffs), new officers
got elected and the food hasn't changed,
at least not according to my grandfather.
"See this?" he says, pointing at the sauce
on his Salisbury steak. "I call it motor oil."

Pee on Your Foot

If you're like me and prone to athlete's foot,
you might pay attention to the clean-cut guy
behind you, who shouts "Pee on your foot!"
before the pharmacist can impart his advice.
But first you might turn around and say,
"What?!"
"It's what we did in the army. Best medicine's
your own urine."

Anyway a story like this, told in advance,
is far better than the three weakest words
in English—*I can explain*—when your girlfriend
finds you standing in the bathtub
with one pant leg rolled up. By *you*
I mean, of course, me, and I hate to think
of what I must look like, more deeply absorbed
in the task at hand than I ever was
reading a Walt Whitman poem—
and I *love* Walt Whitman, who once said,
"If you love to have a servant stand behind
your chair at dinner, it will appear in your writing,"
which is maybe what this is about.

It's easy, when I pee on my foot, to picture
showering alongside my GI buddies
peeing on theirs, in a row of parallel arcs.
Other times, I revisit the thrill of infancy,
where you can let yourself go anytime, anywhere.
There was never any shame till we invented it.

So pee on your foot, people. Do it for yourself,
your country. Do it for Walt Whitman.
Do it for your foot.

Swimming to New Zealand

Once or twice in life you find a woman
you'd swim the ocean for. *What are you doing?*
friends will ask, as you perfect your stroke,
meantime pitying everyone outside of love.
Your only obstacle, the blue Pacific—
where your sun sinks, she's dressing in the morning,
and when the dawn comes reaching back around,
turning up the volume in your city,
she's drawing blinds, removing her make-up.
If you were Gatsby you would build a mansion
in some cove off the Tasmanian sea
and throw parties to lure her in. You're not
of course—though nothing's impossible,
except life without her, and so you swim.

3

Too Soon

Too soon to write a love poem
for a shy girl who won't
tell you on the phone
what she is wearing—
just "underwear."
Too soon to say "girlfriend"
though she likes it
on the lips of others
jumping to conclusions,
like a Frisbee through a window.
Too early for "I love you"—
though no problem with
a punch on the arm, "I'm going
to steal that sweatshirt,"
"You're sort of awesome."
The language of the shy
is full of *maybe,* full of
kind of—"I maybe
kind of miss you a little"—
words to sand down a confession
lest it scratch her underbelly
or bring to boil what she wants
simmering on a burner
or under T-shirt and jeans.
It's premature for nicknames, Sarah
my tomboy (*in panties!*),
Princess *Whatever,* queen of shy,
too soon for a love poem—ah,
but too late for the blackbirds
to get back in the pie.

Shin Issues

Probably you have shins.
If you were born shinless
there would still be *something* between
your knee and ankle and we
could call that space
shin,
just as we could say the unknown guy
who supposedly wrote Shakespeare's plays
was also, coincidentally, named Shakespeare.
That was a long sentence.
We elected a president who has shins.
He stands with other world leaders,
or they sit talking with their shins
parked indifferently under
the table like service dogs.
Let's say you're feeling bad, or else good—
no matter: your shins will still be
only okay. Unless you whack them
on, for example, something.
In that case go ahead and scream why don't you.
"Son of a bitch!" you could shout,
like your father, or just bark.
In closing, you might think of trees
as having shins. They don't.

To a Teacher

for Georges Lopez

You, who had goldfish
older than us, regarded us
as ancient inventions, new stars: people.
I was the shortest, afraid
others were staring at my hiney
as we gathered around the turtle
and learned its ways. We practiced
looping our letters high and round.
We celebrated Flag Day, Arbor Day,
United Nations Day (I was Cuba
in a white undershirt) . You wrote
a 3 in front of a row of zeros, said
that's how many people there are
and then asked us to believe
the impossible: there was only
one of each of us in the world.
Five-year blooms, new travelers
in buckle shoes on line for lunch
where they could have fed us anything.
We may have been accidents,
ant murderers, keepers of messy rooms,
future alcoholics and bank robbers,
but you knew us there,
perched on our toad-stools.
How puzzled we were, in June
when you cried to see us go.

Simple Math

Two plus two will always equal four,
as sure as God made green superheroes.
You don't need to know anything more

when you're little. You'll know the score
when greasy-headed Nicholas Shapiro
says, "Two plus two don't always equal four,"

gazing down at the school bus floor,
"but zero times a million is still zero."
"Well you're stupid," you say, not knowing more.

"Well I heard your parents got you at the store,
along with your adopted brother Theo—
so two plus two of *you* could equal four."

"So what?" you say, "at least we aren't poor,
and we're not a bunch of Jewish weirdos."
But Nicholas isn't listening anymore.

And the bus rolls on like a portable war,
where zero times a million is still zero,
and two plus two will always equal four.
You don't need to know anything more.

Bill

My first Little League manager
was supposedly too young to coach,
just a college kid who wanted a team.
He kept pestering the league
and because there weren't enough
interested fathers they finally gave him
us: the Central Federal Savings Mets.

We loved how we got to call him Bill,
and because he wasn't anybody's father
Bill belonged to us all. And Bill
had a rocket arm, and Bill knew baseball,
and naturally you want to hear how we
became champions, and I want to tell you.
But we stunk. Bill stood clapping

for each of us as we went up to bat,
applauded as we slumped back to the dugout.
And we cheered for him at McDonald's—
where the winning coach was supposed to
treat his team, though we lost every game.
Twice a week, Bill was up at the register
counting out a stack of crumpled ones.

Forgiveness Poem

Lately I've been sad about my old cat,
not because I put him to sleep
but because I waited to do it. The Jets
were finally in the playoffs that year
and while I watched them battle the Patriots,
Roscoe, who hadn't eaten in days
and was now blind, sat trembling
in a corner he'd never occupied before.
The animal hospital was open until five—
I figured I could take him in a cab
after the game, perhaps at halftime
if the trembling got worse. I loved
that the young female veterinarian
didn't even question me, just gave me
papers to sign and asked if we wanted some
time alone, at which point I started bawling.
I loved that I bawled my eyes out,
and kept it up when the needle went in,
and when I peered into the celestial wisdom
of his face I found forgiveness, and when
I walked off carrying the empty carrier
it didn't even matter that the Jets had lost.
I'm not proud of the fact that when I got home
I looked up that veterinarian online
to find out if she was single, and how
she might look without a lab coat—though
I don't think that's actually so terrible.
If anything I've managed to remember
only the mildly terrible, which blocks out

the really terrible, the truly horrible,
which can barely, if ever, be written.

You Could

I stood in the middle of my kitchen eating butter.
It was 11 a.m. on an overcast morning.
I was wearing an undershirt and pajama bottoms.
I don't make a habit of this—I'd never
done it before. It wasn't a whole stick,
though a good half inch. Popped it in
and let it melt into the flesh under my tongue,
the place where you'd insert nitroglycerin
if that's what you needed.
I won't describe the taste—
you'll have to try it for yourself.

Perhaps when you've found yourself
thinking about *goals,* that would be
a good time to let some butter
have a ride on your tongue.
My father wanted to retire by forty
and we all heard that bomb ticking.
Each night before heading to bed, as he
stood at the stove triple-checking the burners,
he could have tried some. Hotel Bar,
lightly salted, I believe my mother bought,
though the brand doesn't matter—
they never need to advertise.

You could stick a thumb in a bowl of icing,
scarf a pie with no hands, like a wolf—
whatever pulls you in from
or shoves you out on the ledge

you might need to come in from or go out on.
You don't have to climb Everest—unless
you find yourself in front of it and
can't come away. Unless something's
calling you to do something your friends
wouldn't understand in a million years.

I don't understand butter.
I know it comes from cows, who
have given so much for so long.
But it's a person I picture, the first to try it.
Others in the tribe discarded the floating globules,
but this one opted to taste the world, the same
world that has us so worried and confused.
Maybe you have heart trouble—
you could still, just once, do it,

and write it down: *Today was overcast.*
I stayed in my pajamas just because.
Oh and I ate butter—incredible!
Long after you died they could find
your journal and say, "This one lived!"
or "What an idiot!" No matter.
You don't have to fly to Paris for chocolate—
though you could—and you definitely
don't need to retire and attend baseball games
in every major league stadium. Instead
you could devote yourself to mastering
the dance sequence in Michael Jackson's "Thriller,"

which is what my UPS driver has done.
What a performance Arnie puts on,
to a beat in his iPod only he can hear.

Elaine!

This love makes me think of *Cinema Paradiso*,
Salvatore standing through the winter
beneath the window of the banker's daughter
waiting for her heart to thaw; or Benjamin
at the end of *The Graduate,* screaming
the bride's name from the back of the church
like a crazed ape, then fending off her family
with the mammoth cross ripped from the wall.
But that kind of thing only works in movies—
in real life I think it's called stalking.
So while I wait for the life in which you love me,
I'll just admire the trees, standing stoically
all winter, as if they didn't have veins and pulses,
as if they aren't gripping the earth for dear life.

Privilege

When my friend became an administrator
and demanded $1000 of a grant
he'd ordered me to apply for
he explained, "I get that."
"What did you expect?"
said another friend, a cynic
I enjoyed until we got tired
of being appalled at one another—
though isn't moral shock
one of the privileges of community?

—a word my father now uses,
though what he means is white people
inside the gates, as in, "I was sad
to see friends leave our community
when the tech bubble burst."
He says financial security means
"everything," yet he worries
about 300 million Chinese
climbing into the middle class.
It was a privilege to witness

Jamel in the jail school
campaigning for pizza I was giving
the boys who'd memorized and recited
Shakespeare's 18th sonnet.
"What makes you think you get pizza?"
I asked this skinny child who'd
performed a home invasion,

duct-taping an old lady to a chair.
He looked at me with big sleepy eyes
and said, "Mista, I *deserve* pizza."

So I included him—he seemed
more sure than me that everyone
on this good earth deserves a slice.
I wish I could tell the difference
between entitlement and sacrament,
when it's right to lose your shirt,
when it's okay to paint the town.
When this fuckin' kid gave me a hug
I knew even less, just that *Rough winds
do shake the darling buds of May.*

Walking a Labyrinth

Eleanor, who is driving
me to the Atlantic
City bus station,

asks if I wouldn't
mind stopping
at a labyrinth

in Longport she hates
to pass. Outside of
mythology, or *The Shining,*

all I know of labyrinths
is that you're supposed
to walk them, slowly.

This one is painted:
white lines
on green asphalt.

Feel yourself emptying,
she tells me
as we meander in,

the countless switch-backs
relieved by long arcs
that deliver us

into new quadrants.
An Hispanic woman
and two little boys

have joined us, but
the boys soon lose
patience, and cut to

the circle in the middle,
where they shove one another
like sumo wrestlers.

When we arrive, I'm not
sure if I've accomplished
anything. I look over

at the Church of the Redeemer,
which is closed, feeling
quietly mocked.

On the way out, Eleanor
tells me, you're supposed
to fill yourself with aspirations,

things you want in your life.
That strikes me
as a little greedy—

though I *would* like
to make my bus.
Eleanor would like

her Bahá'í divorce
to be over with,
the year of living alone

and dating nobody
but her husband.
It becomes hypnotic,

retracing the turns,
the painted lanes...
I look up

and see my mother,
whom I haven't
seen in years,

treading innocently
as anyone
while walking a labyrinth,

or folding laundry,
or driving a child
to the doctor.

You could try
to figure it out,
the pattern of it all,

But it might
be better just
to walk it, slowly.

Telemachus at 50

My father? I'm tired of the subject.
But you keep asking, so here's a story:
when I was small he used to take me sailing
out behind the house in a little skiff.
Each time we reached the mouth of the harbor
I'd stand and point and ask, "What's over there?"
He'd just turn for home without a word.
My father never taught me things that matter—
how to read the trades or trim the sails,
to outrun storms or else steer into them.
I learned haphazardly from old pirates,
gamblers and ne'er-do-wells, and I learned late,
and I never had much of a ship. But somehow
I managed to see the world with my own eyes,
lands where the light itself is a different color,
shining on girls with iridescent skin,
where fruit falls from astounding heights and tastes
peppery, and their gods are full of fiery joy,
and toy-like coins jangle in my pockets
as I keep wandering this amazing world.
No treasure for the heart that stays in the harbor—my
father may have known that—I don't know.
Now you tell me he's near, and proud of me?
He's proud of *who* exactly? And who is *he?*

4

Nameless Boy

1.

My friends didn't name their third child
until they got to know him, far better
I think than parents naming children
from a bible or a daydream or a relative
who died an untimely death, or worse:
after themselves, a sad and selfish act.
But unless they planned to give him
an Indian name like "Weeps at Daybreak"
or "North Facing Duck," or one of those
celebrity child names designed to ruin
a perfectly good noun like *Apple* or *Sailor,*
I didn't understand how they'd recognize
the word the stork forgot to bring.

2.

But I liked the thought of this boy
gazing at the world without concepts
as newborns do, yet somehow in a purer
state of suspension, which I try to attain
each morning in meditation, counting
breaths until I've forgotten my name.
When I went to see the nameless boy
his sister, Maya (named for a Russian skater)
told me she was a snow faerie
and I told her I was a polar bear
and she said she was the queen of the moon
and I said I was the boss of Canada

and she said, *YOU'RE JUST DOUG!*
A triple spondee so gorgeously executed
I felt strangely honored and aptly named.

3.

My first name seems to go with every girl I've met
or might—Doug and Margie, Doug and Mary,
Janet and Doug—while Goetsch goes with none.
Some girls in college decided to call me Doug Wonderful,
perhaps to tell themselves there *is* a Mr. Right.
Are you really Doug Wonderful? said Wendy
as she took off her clothes. There was a time
I entertained changing my name to Gatsby,
though how to avoid the diabolical caesura:
Douggatsby? Any name but mine
for a poet, which sounds like a clerk.
When a writing student put me in a list
of those he saw on higher mountain slopes—
Auden, Bishop, Lowell, Kinnell, and Goetsch—
he didn't insult me, but my name did.
"Darkness, my name is Denis Johnson," said Denis
Johnson in a poem, and the darkness said,
"That's good, as long as you're not Doug Goetsch."
"Who the fuck is he?" said Denis Johnson
and they had a good laugh.
Even if I were a rebel in history
I don't think I'd make the litany
in W.B. Yeats's "Easter, 1916"—

after Connelly, McDonough and McBride,
who wants to visit the slum of Goetsch?

4.

I've always thought it a loving habit of family
to remind you of your name, lest you forget
and shame the clan: *Sophie close your legs
you're a Baumgarten.* Emerging
from the courthouse, a man says
to his boy, *You are Barry Alan Blumenfeld
and don't you forget it!* The Jewish names,
so desperately vacated by stage performers,
contain extra charm when said with pride,
while the ad slogan of a Lutheran—
With a name like Smucker's it has to be good—
always struck me as a strange and daring claim.
And how can we not love demands for justice
based solely on the fact you have a name
pronounceable by your outraged friend—
They can't do that to you, you're Douglas Goetsch!
and suddenly you swell with pride
and see his point, as I once tried
to convey to Harvard University, concluding
my recommendation with the sentence,
We're talking about Sara Cohen, and what
do you know they took her early.

5.

Amazing how a name accompanies
a person over the course of a lifetime,
a baby-faced Billy or Tillie or Kate
tags along from the schoolyard to the altar
to the dialysis clinic, a Jamie, Becky
or Candy hardening with the years.
Type your name into Google and you'll find
a death notice for it. If you ever want
to shed your name, start by avoiding reunions—
because whatever they called you, they were wrong:
the name they stole your lunch money from,
the name they scribbled on the bathroom stall,
the name the crazy girl wrote on the board,
hearts above the i's, arrows through the t's,
the full name on your birth certificate
with which your mother summoned you downstairs
and the young ladies of Italy would later
mangle in their beautiful mouths and you didn't
dare correct them—not Sabrina, not Sabina,
not Francesca, not black-haired Rafaella.

6.

Why is it I can't remember your name?
You told me a moment ago, but I didn't
tie it to anything and now it's sailed out to sea,
so I wait around all night to hear it repeated,
perhaps by you, and if I'm exposed

does it mean we're through? People
call me Greg all the time and I forgive them.
How could I possibly be a Nancy?
said a woman I thought I knew. *Seriously:*
what about me could be construed as Nancy?
When I called Pauline Paula
she said, *Paula? Do I look fat?*
I had a try-out at a restaurant where
the entire wait staff was gay and named Helen.
Don't worry, said one, with a toss of his hair,
you'll soon be Helen too. Up until then
every Helen I knew was stoic, Asian or old,
though I suppose the crew took comfort
in her syllables, hitting hard on "Hell"
then rounding its corner. Hell
is thinking up what to say to your lover
after calling out the wrong name.

7.

What I needed from my mother was not a name,
just a counting of the fingers and the toes
and one other thing: to stay in her gaze forever
as she gazed at me then. My grandmother
wanted a girl, and if she'd gotten her wish
what name would I have worn all these years,
worn like a nightgown slipped into and out of
as easily as Douglas? *I could 'a been a Christina,*
said Marlon Brando, perhaps the most perfectly

named individual ever, alongside Harry Truman,
Judy Garland, Johnny Cash, Joe Namath,
and a student of mine named Jessica Pacifico.
I was the English teacher who got to ask
a girl named Mary Rose if a rose
by any other name would really smell as sweet?
Yes, she answered, because in her
opinion Romeo was a hottie.
I said, *What about Nigel?*
Nigel who?
'Wherefore art though Nigel?' That's who.
I'd still date him.
Egbert?
Not a problem.
Biff? Irving? How about Fenster?
Yes, said Mary Rose, *Yes,* until I said
Hitler—which stunned us all to silence.
In the group home I taught a class of seven girls
named Asia: Starasia, Sha Asia, Shatasia, Shaquasia,
Quanasia, Tarasia, and just plain Asia.
In the jail school My God appeared one day—
that's what it said on the printout. I asked
My God if he had a nickname—*Nope*—
then sat the kid next to Jesus the rapist.

8.

You can't, for names, beat a racehorse—
Foolish Pleasure, Spectacular Bid, Funnycide,

Cardigan Bay, Carry Back, Skip in Place,
Wooda Shooda Kooda, Stevie Wonderboy.
What is it about the paddock or the track
that turns breeders and owners into poets
if only for a word or two between cigar chomps?
Or do they just obey what their pig-tailed daughters
whisper in their ears: "*Oh Daddy please*
call him Firestreak, Spiderback, Rocket Wrangler,
Alysheba, Mistral Sky, Whirlaway!"
Or maybe it's their julep-sipping, silk-dress
mistresses who coax the names from them...
Lady Van Gogh, Royal Infatuation, Casual Lies,
Tom Fool, Party Jones, Blondeinamotel, Ya Late
Maite, Whosleavingwho, You Don't Know Jack.
But the horses have to know there's hope
built into they're names when they round
the final turn into the home stretch,
a hundred thousand voices screaming
Go Man Go! Holy Bull! Buckpasser!
C'mon *Johnny Dial! Down the Brick!*
Doncha Dare! Do Good! Look Busy!
Expectamiracle neck and neck with *Slow Joe Doyle,*
but *Secretariat* is moving like a tremendous machine!

9.

Are we ever more consumed with a word
than when we first approach a city
such as London, Lisbon, Dublin,

Geneva, Jakarta, Vienna? Did the founders
know the poetic freight those syllables would carry
when they arrived on horseback or the deck of a ship
exhausted and dreamy to lift a name
from the mist in their brain for the vista
they beheld—Casablanca, Jerusalem, Shanghai,
Nairobi, Istanbul, Timbuktu?
Even American cities are loaded with birdsong:
Chicago, Atlanta, Winston-Salem,
Boston, Baltimore, Albuquerque.
Can you think of a better sound than Cincinnati,
unless it's Philadelphia? The hard-edged
Akron, Trenton, Duluth, Detroit, Vegas,
take their rightful places, along with the comic
Milwaukee, Sheboygen, Boise, Wala Wala,
Hoboken, Weehauken, and the irrepressible
Cleveland, a word to add humor to any sentence,
as in: *I got a wife in Cleveland and she hates my guts.*
And yet, driving Pennsylvania, who isn't dumbstruck
by the unsavory names of its towns—
Blandon, Bloserville, Scotrum, Scranton—
as if some dark cloud of nomenclature
had descended on Hecktown, Butztown,
Brunnerville, Loyalsock, Lickdale?
Could this have been the work of the Amish
taking refuge linguistically as they do in clothing
drab and ugly, shunning all worldly interest
in Lurgen, Blain, Mertzville, Blanchland,
renaming the new land for a gnawing sadness

they hoped to dispel in Snedekerville?
Is there any doubt the citizens of Intercourse,
Blueball, Letitz, Bird-In-Hand have some explaining
to do to their children at inappropriate ages?
Growing up in Long Island, I rode my Schwinn
on the spiritless grid of suburban dystopia
within the confines of the "M" section,
past stick trees newly planted in farmland
with no great oak or elm or beach
to lend a street a landmark, no storied maples
on Mapleshade Lane, no hill on Mosshill Place,
Millstream Lane running flat and dry
into Millbrook Drive. That's what happens
when you move people into potato fields
and name roads as fast as you lay down asphalt
in towns that sound like soap opera locales:
Valley Stream, Lake Grove, Floral Park.
Nobody was baptized in Wading River.
I never threw a stone in Stony Brook.

10.
It takes a prophet to make a true name,
which is why young Robert Zimmerman
was right to re-call himself. And if you're not
inspired you should at least wait a while,
as my friends did with their third child,
steering past Michael and Brandon, Kyle
and Cody, Justin and Tyler and Ryan, landing

on Dylan, 38th on the list of U.S.
names for boys that year, but I never asked
how they decided, if he spit on his bib and they
read it like tea leaves, or just watched the changing
weather on his face as they turned the radio dial,
though who doesn't arrive sooner or later,
tired and broken, to "Visions of Johanna,"
"Tangled Up in Blue," "Blind Willie McTell"?
Bob Dylan first tried calling himself Elston Gunn,
Jack Fate, and almost went with Robert Allen,
but he liked the sound of Dylan
because, he said, *the letter D came on stronger.*
And if a certain Welsh poet didn't drink
himself to death, he might have hung around
Greenwich Village just nine more years
for some American lyrics to lift him up.
As for my friends' boy, he's ten now,
the smallest kid in Pop Warner Football.
He roots with his life and his death
for the New York Mets, knows more
about the Revolutionary War than his parents,
and if something better ever came out
of Brookfield, Connecticut, I'm not aware of it.
Doug, write a poem about me,
said Dylan Goldweit-Denton, so I did.

NOTES

"Darkness, my name is Denis Johnson" (section 3)
quotes Denis Johnson's poem "Now."

"Secretariat is moving like a tremendous machine"
(section 8) quotes Chick Anderson's racetrack call
of the 1973 Belmont Stakes.

"I got a wife in Cleveland and she hates my guts"
(section 9) quotes the song "Born Too Late," by
Steve Forbert.